HIDDEN TREASURES

ASHFORD

Edited by Allison Dowse

First published in Great Britain in 2002 by
YOUNG WRITERS
Remus House,
Coltsfoot Drive,
Peterborough, PE2 9JX
Telephone (01733) 890066

HB ISBN 0 75433 910 6
SB ISBN 0 75433 911 4

FOREWORD

This year, the Young Writers' Hidden Treasures competition proudly presents a showcase of the best poetic talent from over 72,000 up-and-coming writers nationwide.

Young Writers was established in 1991 and we are still successful, even in today's technologically-led world, in promoting and encouraging the reading and writing of poetry.

The thought, effort, imagination and hard work put into each poem impressed us all, and once again, the task of selecting poems was a difficult one, but nevertheless, an enjoyable experience.

We hope you are as pleased as we are with the final selection and that you and your family continue to be entertained with *Hidden Treasures Ashford* for many years to come.

CONTENTS

Lucy Heuch	32
Rhianna Sauvage	33
Nick Gray	34
Chloe Kendall	35
Tom Adams	36
Melissa Dewar	37
Abigail Brookson	38
Shauni Hardy	39

Furley Park Primary School

William Jarvis	40
Abigail Bundock	41
Sam Hunt	42
Claire Gallagher	43
Jamie Crowe	44
Danielle Newman	45
Hollie Robinson	46
Kraig Crisp	47
Emma Newens	48
Dwyane Tomlinson	49
Alexandra Pares	50
Adam Crick	51
Joe Bee	52
Emma Ghosh	53
Michael Tucknott	54
Luke Newman	55
Wei Jen Lee	56
Laura Butt	57

John Mayne CE Primary School

Max Morgans	58

Kingsnorth CE Primary School

Toni Hurcombe	59
Benjamin Haddon	60
Alexander Merson	61
Shaun Campfield	62
Kristian Matthews	63

The Poems

THE SNOWY OWL

The wise old owl,
As white as snow,
Sits in the broad oak tree.
Two beady, glass eyes stare at its prey
Laying in the waving grass.
With a swift swoop, it descends and clutches
Its terrified prey between its razor-like claws.
Ascending up into the darkening sky,
It returns to the broad oak branch.
Using its saw-like beak, it tucks into its lifeless meal.
Satisfied, it takes a last look around
At the blackness surrounding
And closes its marble eyes as
The dawn of a new day begins to rise.

Harriet Boulden (9)
Aldington Primary School

THE SUNRISE

As the sun creeps round the corner,
The animals start to wake.
The birds are whistling in the trees
When the badgers start to snore.
As the moon goes down to rest
The grass waves good morning.
As the cockerel sings to the sun,
It smiles hello, waving with
Its beautiful sunbeams.

Zoe Bateman (11)
Aldington Primary School

FISH

Fish, you are as quiet as a mouse,
You swim all day and have lots of fun,
You push yourself so fast and slick,
Your streamlined body smooth as felt,
Your scales so flat as pancakes,
Until you're tired now,
So go to sleep until another day.

Tom Chambers (10)
Aldington Primary School

NIGHT

Night is a blanket surrounding us.
Night is a gloomy monster coming to get us.
Night is millions of beetles, like an army protecting us.
Night is big, black eyes following us.
Night is a quiet hush while the sun sleeps over us.
Night is a giant's hand shadowing us.
That's night.

Sophie Peppitt (9)
Aldington Primary School

MY CAT HARVEY!

My cat Harvey thinks he's a bat,
My cat Harvey wears a hat.
My cat Harvey carries a bag,
My cat Harvey is in love with a hag.
My cat Harvey likes to play,
My cat Harvey sometimes plays with clay.
My cat Harvey eats fish,
My cat Harvey makes a wish.
My cat Harvey has a room all to himself,
My cat Harvey has a shelf.
My cat Harvey loves to sleep.

Christine Coker (10)
Aldington Primary School

LUNCH

Sandwiches screech at me,
Crisps punch other crisps,
Penguins squawk at me,
Jammie Dodgers dodge from me,
Frubes wobble angrily,
Satsumas boom at me,
My drink winks at me,
My lunch box crunches at me.
I eat them quickly,
Saying, 'Are you satisfied?'
'Yes, thank you.'

Emily-Rose Rolfe (9)
Aldington Primary School

THE ONE-EYED, BLACK-EYED MONSTER

In a cave with a mouth like a gaping bear,
Lies the one-eyed, black-eyed monster.
His skin as oily as an old petrol can,
His breath is as smelly as old socks
That have been on sweaty feet,
And he only has one eye,
Only one black eye.
He was born with only one eye,
He will die with only one eye.
It is as beady as a beetle,
As black as coal.
It looks as fierce as a lion's eye
But with no pupil.
His feet are as warty as a witch's finger,
His teeth like razor-sharp blades.
In a cave with a mouth like a gaping bear,
Lies the one-eyed, black-eyed monster.
As foul as a crocodile is he.
He is the one-eyed, black-eyed monster,
As foul as can be.

Esme Crofton (8)
Aldington Primary School

FOOTBALL

The droning moan
Of your leather sphere
Lets out a groan
When a boot is near.

You rest in the back
Of a netted goal
Pondering fate in the
Goalkeeper's hold.

You stare about
At the numbered shirts
Whilst the injured
Number thirteen hurts.

It's not my fault
I get kicked around
I'd rather stay and
Hug the ground.

Mitre my name
Umbro my friend
My punctured mate Reebok
Unable to mend.

The referee blows
His deafening whistle
Now comes my time
Of sad dismissal.

I sleep alone
In a dark ball shed
From the powerful kick
Sore is my head.

Jamie Hennessy (10)
Aldington Primary School

BACON

Breakfast ready, bacon marched on the plate,
The egg ran on the plate.
The toast muttered to be buttered,
Tomatoes rolled onto the plate.
Yum, yum, I can't wait.
Sausages sprint to get on the plate,
Beans slide onto the plate.

Rachel Pack (10)
Aldington Primary School

IN THE KITCHEN

Seven o'clock, the kitchen wakes up
Bread runs as fast as possible,
Leaps into the toaster to warm up.
The plates fly on to the table,
Marmite walks from the cupboard,
Marches to the toast.
The knife is in charge of us!

Charlotte Coker (10)
Aldington Primary School

A PENCIL SHARPENER

A wood grinder,
An arm spinner,
A shaving giver,
A deadly saw,
A sharp grater.
A pencil sharpener.

Alex Day (9)
Aldington Primary School

The Sea And The Clouds

The sea sits there as blue as the sky,
But then it evaporates.
The clouds suck up water,
It doesn't matter how much the
Grey, giant clouds disembowel,
It always comes back.

The sea holds friends and it holds enemies.
Sometimes the sea betrays us and
Sometimes it rewards us.
That's what I think the sea and clouds are.

Daniel Mills (10)
Aldington Primary School

DAY AND NIGHT

Sun comes up with the shadows
And lets golden beams flow
To banish all the dark.
Dark is still about
Inside all the moaning corners.
All the rabbits and birds
Praise the sun in exultation.
She rises in the east and sinks in the west.

Then the graceful ballerina.
Wherever she dances, silver follows.
Wherever she looks, silver follows.
Everything is quiet and it seems nothing ever stirs,
Only the moon is shining, unleashing her glory.
The Earth becomes a silver ball
And then it all starts again,
The Earth glows once more.

Nathan Moriarty (10)
Bethersden CP School

THE MORNING

The sun rose up and smiled in the morning,
Gave a yawn as the day was dawning.
The flowers got up from where they lay,
The grass shook off the dew, ready for a new day.

The stream gave a splash and started to run,
The moon waved goodbye now the day had begun.
The trees gave a whisper and started to dance,
The bushes awoke and started to prance.

Everywhere the morning was beginning,
The little birds started their singing.
Everywhere was now happy and warm,
Now that it was finally dawn.

Chloë Chaplin (10)
Bethersden CP School

THE GARDEN

G   arden gate swinging open
A   fter the wind has pushed it.
R   ailings standing still as still,
D   affodils shaking from head to toe,
'E njoy the day!' shout the trees,
'N ight is near.'

'N ight has come!' screams the garden.
I   nside the house things are warm,
G   arden shivering with cold,
H   ow the garden survives the night,
T   rying to keep warm.

Laura Laws (11)
Bethersden CP School

THE SEA, A HIDDEN TREASURE

The sea,
A figure of eternity,
Grasping and pouncing
On the world around it,
Gaping with its waves.
The surrounding beach,
A life form in itself.
Forever glistening,
A silent reflection
On our lives.
Twisting and turning
In the jealousy
Of things more beautiful
Than itself,
But it is beautiful
And its attractions
Go deeper,
To the depths of the world.
It changes constantly,
Like a cloud
Moving across the Earth.
The sea rolls
Away, away,
A friend to all, an enemy to everyone,
It calls upon us,
Calls us to our deaths.

Rosa Pritchard (10)
Bethersden CP School

HIDDEN TREASURES OUTSIDE

My hidden treasures I can see,
A rabbit (nine years old),
A coral necklace from the sea,
An ammonite fossil
And an old photo album.

But more treasures are still for me.
The sunrise and the sunset,
The flowers in the woods
And the roaring sea and golden sand,
The woodland creatures
And fields of corn.

These are all my hidden treasures.

Harriet Drage (9)
Egerton CE Primary School

HIDDEN TREASURES IN MY ROOM

My hidden treasures are . . .
My teddy in the corner,
My favourite rings,
My birthstone necklace,
To name some things.

Hidden treasures are memories in my mind . . .
The engraving on Gran's bracelet,
Her life inside a diary,
The photos in our album
Bring back my gran to find.

These are my hidden treasures.

Bethany Goodright (9)
Egerton CE Primary School

HIDDEN TREASURES

In a dark, dark pyramid,
Dark, funny pictures on the wall,
Mummies wriggling out of their tombs.

In a dark, dark pyramid,
Pointed roofs,
Famous mummies in dark rooms.

In a dark, dark pyramid,
Tutankhamen's still asleep.
Creepy spiders hanging from the ceiling,
Lots of hidden treasures -
Scrolls,
Gold,
Silver,
Hidden treasures in the corner.

Thomas Heathcote (11)
Egerton CE Primary School

A TREASURE CAN BE . . .

What is treasure?
Treasure can be
Something deep down beneath the sea,
A treasure hidden in a wall,
A scroll or even a bowl.
It could be a secret or a noise,
It could be a wooden box,
Or even a dog.
Whatever a treasure can be,
My main treasure is me.

Byron Bovis (10)
Egerton CE Primary School

SEA TREASURE

Deep, deep below the sea,
Crystals, pearls, diamonds,
Whatever we see,
Sharks, dolphins, fish are a glee.

That's the treasure I can see.
The sea,
The fish,
The treasure nobody knows,
Is how life flows.

Simon Labahn (10)
Egerton CE Primary School

HIDDEN TREASURE

Treasure? What treasure?
Who put it there?
Has someone got it?
Who's put it where?
Where is it?

The sea,
The wood,
The desert,
The jungle,
The mountains?

Treasure? What treasure?
Who put it there?
Has someone got it?
Who's put it where?
What's in it?

Coins,
Gold,
Silver,
Pearls,
Old photos,
Teddies,
Old toys?

Treasure? What treasure?
Whose treasure?
My treasure!
Here!

William King (10)
Egerton CE Primary School

HIDDEN TREASURES BENEATH THE SEA

Deep, deep below the sea,
Coral reef I can see.
Floating down, down, down,
I see . . .
Fishes swaying side to side,
Sea horses galloping away to ride.
I see . . .
All the ocean treasures special to me.

Rachel Foad (9)
Egerton CE Primary School

THE TREASURES OF THE SENSES

Sights can be treasures in ways,
Like twisting smoke and dawning days.
The smoke so grey, the sunset pink,
Every sight is special, I think.

I think smells can be treasure,
The odour of lavender brings me pleasure,
The fresh, new smell of sap from a tree,
But to the next subject I shall now flee.

Tastes, oh yes, I love them you know,
Sausages, chips. Waiter! Too slow.
Hash browns, pineapple, beans in a pot,
Actually now, that seems rather a lot.

Noises, good noises, drifting around,
Many of these have already been found.
A rustle of leaves for me is a treasure,
I'd better stop now so I don't chat forever!

Jem Rowe (9)
Egerton CE Primary School

HIDDEN TREASURES

Below the crashing waves
Are hidden treasures,
Treasures never heard of.
Fish of different colours,
Glinting violet-purple, ruby-red and emerald-green,
Pearls for queens, kings and princesses!

The sea is a treasure chest,
Full of gold, gems and silver coins.
All hidden treasures
Below the crashing waves,
Below the crashing waves . . .

Joseph Deane (9)
Egerton CE Primary School

THE SEA'S TREASURES

Plants, plants everywhere.
Which is the treasure?
Where? Where?

Their beautiful petals
Glitter and sparkle.
When? Where?

Just look!
Over there!

Jade Cairns (10)
Egerton CE Primary School

THE SEA'S TREASURES

Deep, deep down, beneath the waves,
You see nothing.
But look closer.
Do you see?
Do you see the water world

Where coral creeps,
Where stingrays sweep the golden floor,
Where seashells lay embedded,
Now do you see?
The colours,
The light, beautiful sights,
Bubbles float to the top.

Do you see the water world now?

Rachel Davison (10)
Egerton CE Primary School

HIDDEN TREASURE

I am a treasure,
You will find me by night.
I am a marble,
A marvellous light.

I am a treasure,
I am a glass sphere,
I am a crescent,
By day, I'm not here.

I am a treasure,
I am a boat
That sails through darkness
And is always afloat.

I am a treasure,
You will see me quite soon,
Maybe tonight
Yes, I am the moon.

Rowan Kirk (10)
Egerton CE Primary School

JEWELS

Woodland flowers are like jewels
Glistening amongst the trees.
Snowdrops are so beautiful,
Glinting like pearls in the spring sunlight.

Woodland flowers are like jewels
Glistening amongst the trees.
Bluebells are so beautiful,
Glinting like sapphires in the spring sunlight.

Woodland flowers are like jewels
Glistening amongst the trees.
Campions are so beautiful,
Glinting like rubies in the spring sunlight.

Woodland flowers are like jewels
Glistening amongst the trees.
Violets are so beautiful,
Glinting like purple stones in the spring sunlight.

All of these are so like jewels,
Glinting and glistening in woodlands.

Charlotte Birch (10)
Egerton CE Primary School

HIDDEN TREASURE

My bedroom is an
Aladdin's cave.
It's full of hidden treasure.

It's full of medals
Shining gold and silver,
Photos full of faces,
Certificates for what I've done.

Some of my favourite
Hidden treasure is lurking
In my drawers and cupboards.

Robert Button (10)
Egerton CE Primary School

MY HIDDEN HOME

My camp is where I like to stay,
The trees as walls, the leaves as carpets.
I have picnics and invite the squirrels,
Between the trees, the birds make nests.

My nature home, for me and the creatures.
When rain appears, the trees will shelter me.
Nobody knows a den is here,
My hidden home doesn't need a key!

Sadie Williams (10)
Egerton CE Primary School

HIDDEN TREASURES BENEATH THE SEA

The whirling waves,
Perfect pearls,
Shining shells,
Flying fish,
Chasing crabs.

The sea's hidden treasures
Are all precious to me.

Lucy Heuch (10)
Egerton CE Primary School

HIDDEN TREASURES

I am a treasure,
Lovely and gold.
I am a boat,
Floating about in the sea.
I am a butterfly,
Lovely and colourful.
I am an angel,
Fluttering about.
I am a treasure,
Lovely and gold,
A secret to behold.

Rhianna Sauvage (10)
Egerton CE Primary School

HIDDEN TREASURES

Pressed flowers in a file
Hidden in the walls,
Rotting under floorboards,
Trying to escape.

The floorboards are rattling,
The walls are starting to crack,
Plaster from the ceiling is falling,
Falling on my back.

The treasures are escaping,
They need to get some air.
They crawl through the air vents
And turn up in the drain.

Nick Gray (10)
Egerton CE Primary School

SEA TREASURES

The blue, blue ocean,
I see fishes, beautiful, colourful,
The sleek, slender skin of a stingray.

All these treasures,
Who put them there?

The blue, blue ocean,
I see seaweed, its green arms waving,
Seashells that sparkle like jewels.

All these treasures,
Why are they there?

Deep ocean, who holds its treasures?
You're here, you're there, you're everywhere.

Chloe Kendall (10)
Egerton CE Primary School

HIDDEN TREASURE

In the darkest places
Of the lightest mind,
A treasure to be uncovered.
What will I find?

Tom Adams (10)
Egerton CE Primary School

HIDDEN TREASURES

A secret hidden
In a pyramid,
Written on the walls.

Whispers in the air
Telling of an island's secret,
Never to be found.

Find the golden clue,
Pick up the pieces
And find the lost key.

These things I treasure.
Secrets deep in mind,
Family and friends.

Melissa Dewar (11)
Egerton CE Primary School

HIDDEN TREASURES

There's hidden treasure
In the world,
Somewhere on there.

Are there medals? No.
Is there a treasure box? No.
So what's down there?

While I'm up here,
There's a sparkle in the sky.
I wonder if there's gold,
Or a secret that I know?
But what's a treasure?
A treasure is a special friend
You can talk to.

Abigail Brookson (10)
Egerton CE Primary School

THE SEA

Waves splash around.
Look, look, do you see?
They glitter, they sparkle,
They wave to me.

Deeper we go,
Down, down, look there.
The beautiful fish
Diving on a sunken ship.

I am the big, blue sea.

Shauni Hardy (10)
Egerton CE Primary School

FROM THE COCKPIT

As I soar above the Earth I see . . .
All the cups that Arsenal have won,
The cat that sits at my feet,
The sheep that roam the world,
The football pitch where footballers score,
All the dogs in the garden having fun,
The playground full in all corners,
The horses running free in their fields,
Birds flying in the air and landing in trees.
I'm free to soar and see anything at all.

Willliam Jarvis (10)
Furley Park Primary School

NIGHT CREATURES

The owls tu-whit, tu-whooing
On the branches in the tree,
The green-eyed cats
Pouncing on their prey,
The long-winged bats
Flapping around and around,
The mice squeaking as they run
Searching the ground for nuts and berries,
The owls tu-whit, tu-whooing.

Abigail Bundock (11)
Furley Park Primary School

WAR

War is terrible and bloody,
In the trenches dark and muddy.
Bullets fly across the field,
A tin wall acts as a shield.
Suddenly, Spitfires roar overhead
And British soldiers shout, 'Shoot them dead!'
The Germans attack with tanks and all,
The bullets fly and thousands fall.
Adrenalin's pumping and artillery flying,
Hundreds of soldiers on both sides dying.
The Allies look up to see Germans flee,
Enemy planes retreat to their stations
Ready to fly new operations.
We shoot, we fire, we bomb, we kill,
Then suddenly the message spreads,
The war is over.

Sam Hunt (10)
Furley Park Primary School

I WISH I COULD BE

I wish I could be like a golden eagle
And fly around the world.

I wish I could be like David Beckham
And win the World Cup.

I wish I could be like Harry Potter
And go to Hogwart's School.

I wish I could be like my mum and dad
And be very successful.

I wish I could be like Julia Roberts
And star in a premier film.

I wish I could be like Roald Dahl
And write many best-selling books.

Claire Gallagher (10)
Furley Park Primary School

BASEBALL

B alls fly fast through the air,
A lways excitement around.
S ounds from people shouting loudly for their team,
E veryone is eating their snacks.
B lue skies overhead,
A lready, ten runs are scored.
L ast man is run out,
L oudly the people cheer for glory.

Jamie Crowe (10)
Furley Park Primary School

MY KANGAROO CALLED LIZZY

My kangaroo called Lizzy
Has bright blue sparkling eyes.
My kangaroo called Lizzy
Goes bouncing around all night.

My kangaroo called Lizzy
Has a big baby called Dizzy.
Dizzy is a funny thing
Who shouts about every little thing.

My kangaroo called Lizzy
Only goes to sleep when she's tired.
My kangaroo called Lizzy is feeling rather sleepy,
My kangaroo called Lizzy is asleep!

Danielle Newman (10)
Furley Park Primary School

THE ZOO

When I go to the zoo,
I see tall giraffes eating leaves,
Big elephants washing themselves
And jumping kangaroos leaping about.
In the afternoon when I'm hungry,
I can smell hot dogs, doughnuts and Coca-Cola,
But at the end of the day,
I have to say goodbye.

Hollie Robinson (11)
Furley Park Primary School

MY MOTORBIKE

I love my motorbike, it is fast,
It is as fast as an F1 car.
If I was a motorbike,
I would go as fast as I could,
With screaming engines that are as fast as a bullet.
I put on my helmet, my shirt and my boots,
Then I start up my engine,
Rev it up, pull in the clutch,
Into gear and speed away.

Kraig Crisp (10)
Furley Park Primary School

THE TOWN

The town is busy, people rushing about,
People pushing and shoving,
The market man shouting, 'Come and get your bananas here,'
The smell of hot dogs and doughnuts fresh,
The shops crowded and packed.
That's what it is like in my town in Ashford.

Emma Newens (11)
Furley Park Primary School

THE TOWN

In the town,
Cars going beep, beep,
People having fun,
Sunlight blazing in the sky.
I like Saturday in my town.

Dwyane Tomlinson (11)
Furley Park Primary School

MY TREASURE

My treasure is neither gold or silver,
Nor buried beneath the sea.
It isn't diamonds, it isn't jewels,
It's a treasure deep inside me.

No one can plunder or steal my treasure,
No one can take it away.
My treasure will always be with me,
It will never go away.

My treasure is my family,
My mum and my dad,
Who care for me, feed me when I'm hungry,
Who love and treasure me.

My brothers, however annoying,
Will always be special to me.
So will all the people who make my family,
Who I love and who love me.

Alexandra Pares (11)
Furley Park Primary School

POCKET MONEY

Every Saturday when I get my money,
It's even better than toast and honey.
After lunch I feel like a treat
With chocolate coating, sounds like a sweet.
I trot down to the shop
But the cost of sweets will make you drop.
A bag of chocolates for 50p,
Dairy Milk is better than nice,
If I had enough, I would buy it twice!
Then I go to my secret base.
Oh I do want a sugary lace.
When suddenly down comes the rain
And I trot back down the lane.

Adam Crick (11)
Furley Park Primary School

THE TOWN

As I get off the bus,
The town is very busy.
People rushing about,
Cars beeping their hooters,
Parents dragging children around the shops,
People barging in and out of doorways,
Traders shouting, 'A pound for yer oranges.'
When I get back to the bus,
The town is quiet.
People are leaving the town
And all the shops are shut.
The car park is emptying.
That's my town, Ashford town.

Joe Bee (10)
Furley Park Primary School

THE EXAM

As the paper was laid on my desk, face down,
I couldn't hear a single sound.
As I turned over the paper
And picked up my pen,
I just wanted the ground to swallow me up.

My brain went dead,
As soon as the teacher said,
'OK children, you may start,'
Then went the bang and thud of my heart.

I wondered if anyone else felt the same.
At last the first step was over,
I'd filled in my name!

Emma Ghosh (10)
Furley Park Primary School

MY DAD, YOUR DAD

'Well, my dad is older,' he says.
'Well, my dad is more fit,' she says.
'Well, my dad has a sports car,' he says.
'Well, so does mine!' she says.

'My dad is rich,' he says.
'My dad has a good job,' she says.
'My dad eats a lot of chocolate,' he says.
'So does mine!' she says.

'My dad has a big bed,' he says.
'My dad has a huge bedroom,' she says.
'My dad is fat,' he says.
'So is mine!' she says.

'But my dad's you're dad,' he says.
'Then you're my brother,' she says.
And they go home to bed.

Michael Tucknott (11)
Furley Park Primary School

IF I WAS A DOLPHIN

If I was a dolphin,
I'd swim gracefully through the sea.

If I was a dolphin,
I'd jump through the air with glee.

If I was a dolphin,
I'd spurt blasts of water from my back.

If I was a dolphin,
I'd glide through the waves just like that.

If I was a dolphin,
I'd fly through the coral reef.

If I was a dolphin.

Luke Newman (11)
Furley Park Primary School

MY MOTHER

My mother is very special to me,
Wherever I go, her love will always be there.
When I am sad, she will cheer me up.
My mother is a precious diamond to me,
But most of all, I love her.

Wei Jen Lee (11)
Furley Park Primary School

SWAN LAKE

At first it was a dark and gloomy night,
But then the moon was shining bright.
The water twinkled like shining stars,
A shadow appeared from under a tree.
It glided slowly across the water,
It was a beautiful, white swan.

Laura Butt (10)
Furley Park Primary School

HIDDEN TREASURES

Under the waves the dolphins sing,
Then I see it glistening -
A ring, a sparkling diamond jewel,
Below the water, calm and still.
I reach out with steady hand,
Cut through the pressure, touch the sand,
Grasp the ring but now, too late,
The ring has fallen to its fate
And drops into an oyster shell.
Gone, but in my memory remains still.

Max Morgans (8)
John Mayne CE Primary School

THE EMPTINESS OF A SHADOW'S SOUL

The abandoned shadow mopes about
Under a yellow orb of fire,
Trying to find happiness once again, like a stray dog
He is left to walk the desolate streets alone
And with no one to talk to.
He searches this desert day and night
To find the person he once belonged to.
No luck has he, but instead bitterness and depression.
Salty tears trickle down his cut and bruised face.
Along the powdery pavement he plods
Like a bear, for near eternity.
The sad and lonely shadow asks for
Someone's help, but is ignored.
Thump! He falls on the floor, too tired to get up,
But still no one notices.
The death of the shadow is overlooked by everyone,
They don't care, they don't even shed
One sorrowful tear.
The shadow was nothing but a dead leaf blowing in the wind.

Toni Hurcombe (10)
Kingsnorth CE Primary School

THE SHADOW'S LIFE

A shadow has a life of darkness and sorrow.
A shadow is a slave to us all.
Wherever we go, it shall follow,
Unable to speak and move on its own.
The shadow lives for all time.
When we die it lives on, never moving,
Never speaking, but we know it is there.
The shadow can never make friends at all
Like we do, it does nothing.
A lifeless being with nothing to do but copy us.
Just a simple reflection of our movements,
A mirror image of our actions.
A shadow is nothing, you can't touch it
You can't feel it, you just know it is there.
A mere shade on the ground, never thinking,
Never able to be severed from you.
The shadow is you. You can try,
But it will never go away.
People take no notice of a shadow,
They do nothing but copy.
It is the same as looking in a mirror,
With much lesser meaning.

Benjamin Haddon (11)
Kingsnorth CE Primary School

THE CHANGE OF A POOR ORPHAN

Searching for his mum the young orphan
Shelters under a tree, for he suffers in winter's bitterness.
With his frozen hand he pulls over his
Chequered coat to keep warm.
He slowly falls to sleep in the night's cold, hoping to wake.
The next day he struggles to keep his frozen eyes open
As sparkles of joy awake him.
A new blanket and new clothes await him,
For it is Christmas.
A big smile reaches his face.
His smile is so happy, he cannot stop smiling,
Yet did he realise his luck had changed?
For in a day's time, a man will take him in
And care for him on the magical day of Christmas.

Alexander Merson (11)
Kingsnorth CE Primary School

NEVER TO BE USED AGAIN

I dig, dig, turn, to put a plant in the hole,
I get mud up my spikes.
My owner tosses me in the cupboard
Never to be used again.
But one autumn day, my owner picks me up
To dig a hole for a tree.
Now I'm back in the gloomy old cupboard,
Now I won't be able to see the boiling sun again.
I get taken out. I see the sparkling sky and the red sun.
I get put in the dump van, I get tossed around,
Snapped and a tear trickles down my spike.
I see a burnt out spade, I feel it's me,
Burnt out and worn out.
I get tipped out in a yard full of rusty, old unwanted spades.

Shaun Campfield (10)
Kingsnorth CE Primary School

THE NEW AND THE OLD

A rusty, battered skateboard rolling down the shaggy hill,
Like a beaten child rolling down the hairy hill in a trash can.
Brown-lipped, blood trickling on thy hard face,
Running along on thy stony floor.
They should have drawn me by my bleeding lip.
Young skateboard, sat on the bare floor,
Watching thy brother open his new scooter.
Some songs, some mirth as they watch.
Jealous mind disturbs this laughter,
Pausing at times to have some food and drink,
Or sit by the fire eating sponge cake.

Kristian Matthews (11)
Kingsnorth CE Primary School

SNOW ON THE STREETS

In the winter months the old, crabbed man
Hobbles from one street to the next.
He is waiting for a family to welcome him
Into their warm, cosy house.
How many more days does he lay out
In the cold with his fellow men?
As he steps over his friends, he thinks,
Then out comes a man and says,
'Come into our home and sit in a
Great armchair by our blazing fire.'
Old man Snow couldn't refuse,
So he wiped his muddy feet and
Saw three children with a book,
Candy, and a present each.
The old man sat down
Because it was the day of Christmas.
He left, alone.
Here comes spring!

Nicholas Rayner (10)
Kingsnorth CE Primary School

THE EYE OF THE STORM

The weather-beaten, jagged but distinctive
Outraged rocks, raging and intense,
Quivering shocks propelling waves here and there.
An exasperated, penetrating hurricane
Causing excruciating pain.
Rummaging through the sand and tempestuous water,
Its myopic bolts reverberating down furiously
Like missiles from the Great War!
Boom, down from the vague, cloudy, foggy, misty sky
The rain pummels furiously against the helpless window.
Then suddenly, *boom! Boom! Boom!*
The tempestuous storm stops.

The eye of the storm is over,
But its presence still lives on.

Daniel Fiore (11)
Kingsnorth CE Primary School

THE RACE TO THE END OF THE WEEK

As they plod around the corner, Monday is in front,
He brings a new school and workday in tow,
A depressed male, like an injured animal.
As Monday strides off, shy Tuesday steps into the limelight.
She brings dark evening football matches,
With crowds as big as the pitch.
Tuesday steps off and a new male walks on,
Bringing the midweek day.
Wednesday by name, day by nature.
Soon it's time for him to depart and a new day to pace in.
Thursday leads in the penultimate day
And a cold, murky day with a nip in the wind.
Friday brings the end of the week,
With better educated schoolchildren.
Saturday arrives - a day off for some people.
Following him comes traffic congestion,
Like a blocked up pipe.
Soon Sunday disembarks,
Bringing the day of rest.
People in front of fires as if it was a cold day.
Now the race is over,
It's time for them to go,
For soon, Monday will take the lead again.

Ben Vincer (11)
Kingsnorth CE Primary School

A Leaf Has A Life Of Hope

The winter wind howls like a fox
Through the twisted branches of the bare tree
As the last helpless leaf plunges to the white ground
With a rapid speed that never decreases,
It lays comfortably until with a loud *crack*,
It is trampled on by a man, old and hunchbacked,
But the man just carries on through the swirling mist and the
                                                        drifting snow.
Blue as a sapphire and wrinkled as a cotton shirt
At the bottom of the laundry,
He goes on and on, but the leaf just lays in wait,
For he is weak, small and hurt, waiting for warmth and love.
It lays for days and days watching the world go by,
Watching the children and their loving parents pass with happy faces,
Seeing children open presents by a high, heaped hearth,
But as the leaf's dream slowly fades out of the picture, his
                                                        weakness develops.
It gets weaker each day until the disastrous day pounds upon it.
At twelve midnight, when the snow had fully melted,
The vulnerable leaf faded out of the picture!
(Fortunately, the leaf family will not go completely out of
                                                        the picture,
For photosynthesis creates new plants and a new generation begins.)

Luke Goodsell (10)
Kingsnorth CE Primary School

THE LONELY POUND

Jingle, clink, clash! I hope it's my turn, he thought.
But the lonely pound stayed in the machine.
His shimmer face is the best around.
So why not choose me? I'm as good as new! he thought.
But just then, a thin, wrinkly hand reached out for his face
And lifted him out to a different place.
The pound was astonished, it was black all around him,
For the pound had begun its journey in the black leather bag.
He was jingled and fiddled and clattered about,
His poor little face began to get dizzy.
His mind became angry like a wild bison about to stampede,
He wished he hadn't left his empty dwelling.
Then he was dropped, he didn't know where.
It was the cash machine!
His mind became calm,
Because his journey was over for another day.

Edward O'Donnell (10)
Kingsnorth CE Primary School

The Unhappy Football Pitch

I feel like I've been stabbed four thousand times.
Gigantic, studded boots stamping up and down my back all day.
In the summer I'm very warm,
But freezing in the winter.

I'm extremely lonely here
All on my own.
I have no friends,
I get so bored laying here.

I get a drink sometimes,
But never fed.
My hair gets cut once in a while.
I hate being a football pitch.

Samantha Hensman (11)
Kingsnorth CE Primary School

A Day In The Life Of A Football

Bang! Ouch! You didn't have to kick me so hard.
I sail through the air like a hawk into the back of the soft net,
The goalie picks me up and boots me to the other end of the pitch.
The crowd cheers and the noise is deafening.
The pitch is very long. Wow, I'm going very fast.
A player comes towards me and goes for the goal,
He shoots, he scores!
The other goalie kicks me in the air.
Wow, I'm really high. I can see birds.
I land back down on the ground with a thud.
The whistle blows and lets out a shrill blast.
Ouch, my ears! He picks me up and puts me in the dark,
Horrible place they call a cupboard.
I had better get some rest for tomorrow's match.

Stephen Marsh (10)
Kingsnorth CE Primary School

THE LONELY SHADOW

The miserable day makes him cry,
But no one can see his tears.
He looks for happiness but fails.
The unhappy shadow lurks around the streets
Searching for his place in the world.
He finds a little boy,
But this child has a shadow.
The shadow has no friends or family, just himself.
Full of sorrow, he dawdles into a dark and misty alley
Where he thought he belonged.
The shadow cries once again,
As if he is making a miniature sea.
He cries for the last time
As he slowly dies.

Charlotte Tritton (10)
Kingsnorth CE Primary School

THE ALL-SEEING EYE

The all-seeing eye ricochets through alleyways,
Spying from person to person.
The miserable past, the puzzling present and the promising future
Are all scented by the core of its vision.
Yet he does not run off his own mind,
He searches people's thoughts and feelings,
All of which belong to the spirit of his master.
As the people of Earth leave their planet for better things,
The eye cheers with his master.
Though their work is not done,
They keep travelling on to avenge the galaxy.

Joseph Davies (11)
Kingsnorth CE Primary School

THE SHIMMERING SEA

Slowly moving up and down the warm sand
Collecting shells as I go,
The scorching sun sizzling down on my side,
The palm trees making a reflection on my shiny surface,
The coconuts falling down making a *splash* on me.
A small marine fish swims too far and
Gets stranded on the sand, so I make my biggest wave
And save that red and blue marine fish from that sandy grave.

Danielle Swan (11)
Kingsnorth CE Primary School

JANUARY'S DOWNFALL

A frigid, stony, old lady sits on her dewy throne.
The dreary, amber-brown leaves fall from a sudden ghostly wind.
Frozen, clear ponds are scattered everywhere by a magic spell,
The feeble hands of this lady grab a grey, heavy cloud and
A downfall of rain comes again and again and again.
The hail falls like a million tennis balls all falling at the same time,
The old, argumentative lady fights to see the sun gone
And a dull, grey day is left, just floating. Floating.
The fierce and fighting lady tramples on any colourful
Spring flower that she sees,
Frosty pavements are as slippy as a new bar of soap,
Hills are white with snow as she passes by.
Finally, the winds die down and February comes again.

Laura Grimes (11)
Kingsnorth CE Primary School

THE WHIPLASH STORM

The dew falls to the superior deck like a mother
Enfolded to her newborn baby.
All six crew members have the imagination of a herd of elephants,
But in their wait, an agonising muddle sweeps the
Tattered superior deck of the boat and into the lingering sea.
The boat stays motionless for a few seconds
While the crew wait in silence, then suddenly everything and
Everyone has a short, but sensational experience of
All the wind's might as the boat gyrates round the island,
Gradually sinking further and further down.
To make sure he has final victory, he makes a flash of lightning
As the whiplash storm moves on for another day.

Benjamin Clements (10)
Kingsnorth CE Primary School

THE SUN'S LIFE

A warm summer's morning and the sun's out.
Sun as happy as can be, shining down,
But he wishes he could play with the children.
He starts to get sad.
Children jumping about with the sun on them.
Then he realises that they have fun when he's out.
He starts to get brighter and happier,
But then he realises that he does play with them.
Children jumping like kangaroos in the sun,
People having picnics,
The sun shining brightly is as happy as can be.

Anna Bagulay (10)
Kingsnorth CE Primary School

THE BREATHTAKING STORM

The hysterical storm tatters like a resentful giant,
As thrashing lightning bolts strike the ground
And hailstones clonk the incensed man's govel.
The vines of crystal-clear ice cling to the rooftops
While the rain's building up a flood.
Rustling brown and bright leaves crunch under the capacious boots,
And wind pipes whistle through the ears of the titan.
As the emotionless ogre dwindles into the distance
And the abominable storm starts to fade,
His commodious shadow won't go out of the picture
Because of the colossal height of his figure.
Pitter-patter, what's left of the rain drips from the stratosphere
And again, the high flood fleets down and
The storm passes on for another day.

Sam Osborne (10)
Kingsnorth CE Primary School

THE STORM IS COMING

Whoosh goes the wind, door to door like a swimmer
Trying to catch up with the team.
Angrily shouts a mother hoping her children
Would come into the warm, cosy house.
Bang goes the lightning, coming down all gold and shiny,
Trying to hit something like a tiger running for its prey.
At the seaside the rocks with shimmering shocks
Start to crumble down to the ground
Like toast coming out of a toaster.
As the small, small boats come into the bay they
Sway in the ghostly, cold air.
The tall, strong, lifeguard sits waiting for a chance to swim,
But if he did, he would freeze.

Jordan Cook (10)
Kingsnorth CE Primary School

A Competition In The Life Of A BMX

I'm a BMX spinning through the air
Like a helicopter's rotor blades.
Grinding up boxes, rails and half-pipes,
Hearing crowds roar at backflips and jeer at crashes
And jump up from their seats at monstrous front flips, 'Wahey!'
And then *crash!* 'Boo!' I earn respect from fans by
Landing 360° tail whips, 180° rocket-airs and tabletop backflips.
Flying through the air with 180° supermans
I use grinds like peg-grinds, smith-grinds and
Many more flying tricks, until my turn is over
And I wait for another chance to prove myself.

Daniel Smith (11)
Kingsnorth CE Primary School

THE KING OF WINDS

The ravenous wind charges like a resentful giant
Too enraged to care about how he hits.
Moving promptly from street to street,
Belting people off their feet,
The giant blowing with all his might,
Shrieking with all his rage,
Damaging and wrecking everything in sight,
Invisible he is, but devastating powers he has.
A cold, drizzly breeze is he,
Debris being chucked out of his fists,
Howling through towns and cities like a hungry werewolf.
As day turns into night,
The tired giant starts to lose its powers.
Now the wind is dreaming,
Getting ready for the next stormy day.

Dominic O'Donnell (10)
Kingsnorth CE Primary School

THE LIFE OF THE SEASONS

An adventurous boy holding the cold, winter snow,
Holding a hand as he walks over the frozen green grass.
There's the enemy! As he throws, he lost his grandfather
In a winter wonderland of snow.
He staggers to get home.
Then a blizzard domes like a stampede of old winter
Rushing to the old people's home as a hint of light
Peeked out from the cloud,
Then everybody cried, for old winter is now in a grave
And tears are now happy as spring is born,
For he makes everything wonderful as he learns.
He watches over us as we do things.
Time goes on and before you know it,
Everybody's out playing and spring moves to summer.
As summer is running on, he holds that cold ice cream.
As it melts, it attracts bees.
Out of nowhere, those big clouds with thunder and winds,
As helpless little leaves flutter down for autumn is now frosty.
Winter has struck like a knife thrashing at a weak old vegetable.
Winter trying to get home before it's too late.
Then it went black. He had to pass out some day.

Alexander Green (11)
Kingsnorth CE Primary School

OUR HEAD TEACHER

Nobody knows what she's up to in that little room.
She might be sleeping in a tomb,
She might be playing on a Game Boy.
I bet she's got a big bunch of toys.
She might be a spy
Working for the FBI.
Cameras everywhere,
Even on the jumpers that we wear.
If she goes out today,
Nobody knows where she might stay.
She runs around a lot today,
She might arrest someone far away.
Nobody knows what she's up to in that little room.

Charlotte Keedens (10)
Kingsnorth CE Primary School

OUR HEAD TEACHER

What do you think she's up to?
Having a party,
Playing football,
Telling secrets,
Spying on us,
Playing darts,
Telling us off,
Drinking beer and eating chocolates?
What is she like?

Sometimes bad-tempered,
Out of this world,
Cheeky,
Sense of humour,
She takes control of the whole school.
She hasn't retired yet.

Lauren Ring (10)
Kingsnorth CE Primary School

OUR HEAD TEACHER

Our head teacher stays after school.
She nicks our crisps,
She nicks our toys,
What is she up to? Drinking alcohol maybe?

Our head teacher parties at night.
She watches cartoons,
She plays mini-golf,
What is she up to? Smoking cigarettes maybe?

Our head teacher plays at amusement parks.
She puts cameras up,
She plays on her Game Boy,
What is she up to? Playing mini-darts maybe?

Ashima Dewulf (10)
Kingsnorth CE Primary School

OUR HEAD TEACHER

Our head teacher stays locked in a room,
What could she be doing?
Has she got a pony which she rides
Along the beach,
Or does she press a shiny red button
And a golf course comes up?
Could she be a child in disguise
And go off down the park,
Or maybe does she have a cute little puppy
That she plays with?
Or is she a spy for the FBI
And has cameras everywhere?
I don't know - you have to think!

Rebecca Buck (9)
Kingsnorth CE Primary School

IN TROUBLE

I'm in trouble, time is ticking.
Wish I never did it.
Hope it goes quick!
Hope it goes fast!
Why did I do it? What's gonna happen?
I've never been here before,
Never even wanted to come here.
I was getting hotter,
I was getting colder,
Wish I'd never done it, wish I'd never done it.

Tap-tip, tap-tip,
Oh no, here she comes!
Wish I'd never done it, wish I'd never done it.
My heart is pumping.
I close my eyes and imagine the worst,
Being expelled!

Wish I'd never done it.
As I slowly open my eyes, I see her.
She enters her office and beckons me in.
Wish I'd never done it.
She tells me that I've done wrong!

Alexander Hickman (10)
Kingsnorth CE Primary School

IN TROUBLE

He saw the clouds above him,
There was tarmac all around,
A school window was broken
And his ball was on the ground.

The head was storming over,
He'd seen the window crack,
He did what teachers shouldn't do,
Smack! Smack! *Smack!*

He was taken to the office
Where he was shown again,
The picture of his teacher
Hitting him with a cane!

Eleanor Brittain (10)
Kingsnorth CE Primary School

CATS

My cat is there when I feel bad,
Times when he's not, I feel sad.
He's always there to comfort me,
He even drinks my cup of tea.

When he goes out at night
I hope he's safe without light.
When he comes in in the morning,
I always end up yawning.

In the middle of the day
He always comes in to play.
When he thinks he's had enough,
He sits down and starts to puff.

Alexandra Hesketh-Wells (9)
Kingsnorth CE Primary School

A To Z Of Football

A is for Arsenal who finish second,
B is for Bradford who are in Division One,
C is for Chelsea who've got foreign players,
D is for Derby who escape relegation,
E is for England, they're in the World Cup,
F is for Football, without it where would you be?
G is for Gillingham, they're in the middle,
H is for Hartlepool, they're in Division Three,
I is for Ilic who used to play for Charlton,
J is for Jerusalem who have got their own team,
K is for Kelly who plays at the back,
L is for Liverpool who win all the cups,
M is for Manchester Utd who always win,
N is for Newcastle who are in the top ten,
O is for Overmars who plays for Barcelona,
P is for Portsmouth who will sack their manager,
Q is for Quebec, they never get far,
R is for Riise who's playing for Liverpool,
S is for Sunderland who do quite well,
T is for Turkey, we beat them 2-0,
U is for Unna who plays for Newcastle,
V is for Varga who plays at the back,
W is for Wrexham, they are slipping,
X is for Xavi who isn't in England,
Y is for Yugoslavia, they're not very good,
Z is for Zambrotta who is Italian.

Fraser Harrison (9)
Kingsnorth CE Primary School

SCHOOL BULLIES

'You've got dirty hair,'
Said Claire.
'You have got a big nose,'
Said Rose.
'You've got a big mouth,'
Said Ralph.
'You smell,'
Said Michelle.
'And you're a pain,'
Said Wayne.
'He is our mate,'
Said Kate.
'You're going to pay,'
Said Ray.
'You're just bullies,'
Said Billy.
'I'm telling the head,'
Said Fred.
'You're in big trouble,'
Said Mrs Bubble.
'We all hate a bully,'
Said Mrs Woolly.
'Your parents will be told,'
Said Mrs Bold.
'And we will find you extra work,'
Said Miss Quirk.

'Bullying never pays
And we will see the error of our ways.
It will not happen ever again,'
Said Claire, Rose, Ralph, Michelle and Wayne.

Jamie Lukehurst (9)
Kingsnorth CE Primary School

THE MOON

The moon twinkles bright,
Sometimes full, sometimes half,
Still beaming at night.
It glitters and shimmers with stars alight
To guide us the way all through the night.
The moon shines happily in the sky
Whilst children dream of merry delights,
From dusk till dawn it glitters above,
Arise the sun, our new day has begun.

Ellie Fiore (8)
Kingsnorth CE Primary School

FIREWORKS

Watching fireworks on a frosty night
I see some curly-wurly,
Frizzy-whizzy, glittering fireworks.
There's one that sparkles like a sparkler,
And curls up in the air,
Whizzy ones whooshing about your head.
There's a swirly one melting the ice,
It makes a *crack, crack, crackle* sound!

Elysia Green (8)
Kingsnorth CE Primary School

HIDDEN TREASURES

Quite deep in the sea
Hidden treasures are waiting
Under the cold sea.

Charlotte Harrison (8)
Kingsnorth CE Primary School

HIDDEN TREASURE

Down below the deep, blue ocean
Are soft, slimy, scaly, salty sharks
That are followed by slimy fish.
Beneath the coral is a slippery, slimy snake.
Inside salty seaweed,
Little fish are swimming about.
The gloomy, old, oozing, oval-like octopus
Is guarding glittering, glistening, great
Golden, gold jewellery.
A crusty crab passed the
Overgrown, seaweed-covered chest
On the old, crusty deck.

Amy Bray (8)
Kingsnorth CE Primary School

HIDDEN TREASURE HAIKU

The hidden treasure
Is under the deep, cold sea,
Waiting to be found.

Nicolle Sims (8)
Kingsnorth CE Primary School

HIDDEN TREASURE HAIKU

Where is the treasure?
Look! There's the hidden treasure.
The treasure is found!

Nathaniel Harmer (8)
Kingsnorth CE Primary School

GUARDED HAIKU

Guarded is treasure
Under the depths of the deep,
Now found in the sand.

Demi Sawyer (9)
Kingsnorth CE Primary School

HIDDEN TREASURE HAIKU

She searches for the
Hidden treasure under the
Ocean far below.

Olivia Brimsted (9)
Kingsnorth CE Primary School

SILLY FISH

Deep below the water is a soft, silly,
Squirmish and slimy, yellow fish.
Now there is a crusty, cranky crab creeping out
Of the old, smelly, shiny, shimmering, shipwrecked ship.
In the ship there is a rusty chest with treasure inside.
There are red, blue and yellow diamonds
With glittery bits on them.

Hannah Nutley (8)
Kingsnorth CE Primary School

HIDDEN TREASURE

Under the deep, blue sea
Is a golden, glittering, glistening great
Green goblin coming to get me.

Thomas Yerrall (8)
Kingsnorth CE Primary School

HIDDEN TREASURE

In the deep, blue waters
A sly, slithering shark
Smiled at me
With its shiny, sharp teeth!

Adam Green (8)
Kingsnorth CE Primary School

HIDDEN TREASURE CHEST

Down in the deep blue sea
A cranky, cold chest is covered
By a creepy, crusty crab.

Helen Vincer (8)
Kingsnorth CE Primary School

HIDDEN TREASURE

Deep in the sea is a chest full of
Glittering, glowing, glorious gold.
Sparkling gold,
Singing in the sun
Breaking through the sea.

Samuel McGee (8)
Kingsnorth CE Primary School

GUARDED OCTOPUS

Down fifty metres below the ocean
There is a carved, curious, careful, crusty chest
Guarded by an old, oval-like octopus.

Anna Flockett (8)
Kingsnorth CE Primary School

HIDDEN TREASURE

In the deep, blue sea
There's a chest
Guarded by a shiny, old,
Sly, slimy, slithering shark!
Swish, swosh, swish.
Swosh, swish, swosh.

Lisa Gamble (8)
Kingsnorth CE Primary School

HIDDEN TREASURES HAIKU

Underwater in
The cold, deep sea on a deck
Are treasures hidden.

Alex Bagnall (8)
Kingsnorth CE Primary School

HIDDEN TREASURE

In the sparkling sea I see a chest
In a secret place guarded by an octopus down below.
The secret place is a shipwreck with seaweed
Coming down from the door.
Inside the chest there is great, glistening gold
For you and me.

Andrew Brittain (7)
Kingsnorth CE Primary School

HIDDEN TREASURE

Down below the deep, blue sea
An old, obedient,
Oval, obese,
Oblivious
Octopus lies guarding treasure!

Leena Kang (8)
Kingsnorth CE Primary School

SEA WORM

Right at the bottom of the sloppy sand
There is a slimy sea worm
Wriggling around.

Danny Mapp (7)
Kingsnorth CE Primary School

THE OLD STEAM TRAIN

Every day people walk on to me like I'm a bit of rubbish
And the drivers throw coal into my heart.
Every day it gets heavier and heavier and the
Humans throw rubbish on me like I'm just a rubbish dump.
Then I see a stop sign and stop as quickly as I can.
The drivers shout at me, like I'm their slave and
They start throwing coal into my heart.
When the humans have all finally gone out,
I feel like it's Christmas, but then
The doors open and people start marching in.
I start to cry while the drivers are shouting at me
And throwing coal into my heart.
I start going again and feel like it's going to be
Better this time, but it all happens again.
At around 9 o'clock, people spray graffiti on my windows.
I only get treated well once a year when
I'm cleaned by the cleaners and I think that it's
Going to be better in the morning, but it starts all over again.

James Thomas (10)
Kingsnorth CE Primary School

HIDDEN TREASURE

Deep in the sea
There's a slimy, sandy,
Slippery, shiny, skinny,
Stinky seaweed.

Natasha Hamblin (8)
Kingsnorth CE Primary School

HIDDEN TREASURES

Under the sea
There is an old, oval,
Oozing, offering octopus
Guarding the treasure.
Never found, forever hidden.

Alex Cox (8)
Kingsnorth CE Primary School

HIDDEN TREASURES

I treasure my computer.
You prefer the TV.

Your sporting talent is a hidden treasure.
I show that I just fall.

You are good at work in the class.
I will just turn away and get things wrong.

You are good at rounders, I get out,
Whereas you win them.

You are good at art, it is a hidden treasure,
But I just scribble and colour badly.

You are a good friend,
I don't think I am.

You made me laugh,
I can't do that. You are a hidden treasure!

Sam Morgan-Smith (10)
St Teresa's RC Primary School

HIDDEN TREASURE

I treasure my chocolate,
You prefer jellybeans.
I treasure cricket,
You prefer tennis.
I treasure my jewellery,
You prefer make-up.
I treasure my cat,
You prefer your hamster.
You are good at ballet,
I'm like a clumsy elephant.
You are good at telling jokes,
I couldn't make a hyena laugh.
You are good at singing,
I couldn't sing to save my life.
You are good at climbing trees,
I can't get past the first branch,
I can't stand up.
Your drawing talent is a hidden treasure,
I just doodle cartoons.
Your dancing talent is a hidden treasure,
I couldn't dance for a toffee.
You're talented in playing the flute,
I can't play a note.
Your reading talent is a hidden treasure,
I take forever to read a page.
Your painting talent is a hidden treasure,
I can just about paint a moon.

Sarah Quinn (10)
St Teresa's RC Primary School

HIDDEN TREASURE

I treasure my precious flute,
You prefer loud pop music.

Your brainy talent is a hidden treasure,
I show my artistic talent.

You are good at fabulous sport,
I can kick a ball and enjoy a good dance.

We both have a hidden talent at dance,
I must agree it's a nice little treasure,

But our best hidden treasure
Is our care and love for each other.

Your caring talent is a hidden treasure,
I suppose I show caring too.

I wonder what your other hidden treasures are?

Philippa Wall (11)
St Teresa's RC Primary School

HIDDEN TREASURE

I treasure my penknife,
You prefer cooking knives.

Your cooking talent is a hidden treasure,
I show that I can't cook.

You are good at woodwork,
I'm hopeless at woodwork.

You are cool at pretending,
I'm just mental in the head.

Your eyes look determined,
Mine show scared feelings.

You are good at sport,
I'm not as good as you.

You are good at helping me,
I can't do as well as you.

You are superb at Airfix models,
I am not as good as you.

You are good at horseriding,
I have never done it.

You are cool at pool,
I am not so good.

Your hidden treasure is *jokery.*

Matthew Saunby (10)
St Teresa's RC Primary School

HIDDEN TREASURES

I treasure my golden locket,
You prefer your silver bracelet.

Your diving talent is a hidden treasure,
I show that I sink.

You are good at making me laugh,
I'm a joke myself.

You are good at scoring goals,
I'm blocked all the time.

You are good at swimming 1000 lengths,
I'm just left behind.

You are good at making things,
I'm just breaking mine.

You are good at winning races,
I'm always fourth or fifth.

Your artistic talent is a hidden treasure.

Nicola Clark (10)
St Teresa's RC Primary School

HIDDEN TREASURE

I die in maths tests,
You steam ahead with answers.
I sit back and get everything wrong
And you run up and get everything right.
I can't swim very far,
You can swim to the ends of the Earth.
I get angry very easily,
You stay as calm as anything.
I can't stand my brothers,
You seem to get on fine with your brother, by some miracle.
I can't go on writing,
But you take pleasure in it.
I don't know what to play with you,
But you always know what to play with me.
I don't know what you think of me, but I like you a lot anyway.

I treasure all these things about you
Because you're my best friend, Sam.

Matthew O'Donoghue (10)
St Teresa's RC Primary School

HIDDEN TREASURE

I treasure my expensive golf clubs,
You prefer your smart football boots.
Your drawing talent is a hidden treasure,
I show total scrappiness.
You're wicked at cricket,
I'm so bad my nan could beat me.
I treasure my heavy metal pop music,
You prefer your slow and calm pop music.
Your constructing talent is a hidden treasure,
I show total destruction.
You're brilliant at swimming,
I get puffed out after about 16-20 lengths.
I treasure my gorgeous Arsenal kit,
You prefer your disgusting Man U kit.
Your singing talent is a hidden treasure,
I sing worse than a cat.
You're excellent at being organised,
I'm extremely *dis*organised.
I treasure my Linkin Park CD,
You prefer your Limp Bizkit CD.
All my friends are hidden treasures.

Daniel Gladwin (10)
St Teresa's RC Primary School

MY HIDDEN TREASURES

I treasure my blue, shiny bike,
You prefer your dull, black PlayStation.

Your clever talent is a hidden treasure,
I show that I look up to you.

You are good at football,
I just can't tackle people.

You get lovely, hot school dinners,
I get cold and strange sandwiches.

I like your comical sense,
That is why I like you.

My hidden treasures I can't show,
But yours is just you.

Your speedy running far,
Will always be better than mine.

Your friendship is a hidden treasure.

James Porter (11)
St Teresa's RC Primary School

HIDDEN TREASURES

I treasure my friends,
You prefer girlfriends.

Your running talent is a hidden treasure,
I show I just fall.

You are good at making jokes,
I can't crack a smile.

When you kick a ball it goes in the net,
I always miss and trip.

My crazy rock music drives you mad,
You'd rather have hip and mellow.

Instead of rounders, which you like,
I'd rather watch wrestling and boxing.

You are really brainy, rather smart,
I always crack up and fail.

I can't remember things, I'm a muddle,
You have things planned out and smooth.

I act like a child, but quite willing and fun,
You're always an adult and hardly are mad.

You always eat chocolate but never get fat,
But when I eat it, it's like eating lard.

When I'm nearly cracking a smile,
You and your wit will stop me by a mile.

Your reading skills would do me in,
I've finished one, you've finished ten!

Even though I'm not perfect, that's a hidden treasure.

Michael Hogan (10)
St Teresa's RC Primary School

HIDDEN TREASURE

I treasure my bestest friend ever,
You prefer me.
You show your marvellous talents,
I am too shy to show my talents.
You prefer your wonderful swimming,
I love my athletics,
I love to run around the field.
You love doing your swimming lengths.
You prefer your artistic drawings which look out to the world,
I do think my drawings are OK, but they don't shine out to the world.
I treasure everything in my life,
You prefer your loving family.
Is kindness your hidden treasure?

Mikumme Posner (10)
St Teresa's RC Primary School

HIDDEN TREASURES

I treasure my pair of old jeans,
You prefer your designer labels.

Your listening talent is a hidden treasure,
I just get bored and fiddle.

You are good at helping,
I am good at needing help.

You are great at running fast,
I'm slower than an injured slug.

I draw a log cabin in art,
You draw Buckingham Palace.

I knit a pair of odd socks,
You knit a beaded cardigan.

I treasure my friend's forgiveness and patience,
My friends treasure me, although I don't know why.

Friendship is a hidden treasure.

Bethany Gogarty (11)
St Teresa's RC Primary School

HIDDEN TREASURE

I treasure my clothes,
You prefer your old teddy.

Your singing talent is a hidden treasure,
I show that I go out of tune.

You are good at dancing,
I have two left feet.

I don't do much at all,
You do everything.

I spend, spend, spend,
You save up for a rainy day.

I'm as hot as a chilli,
You're as cool as a cucumber.

You're good at football,
I can't kick a ball at all.

You're full of talent,
I want to be like you.

You have hidden treasures,
I want some too.

Natalie Summers (11)
St Teresa's RC Primary School

HIDDEN TREASURE

I treasure my cuddly hamster,
You prefer your make-up.

Your singing is your hidden treasure,
I'm still better at dancing.

You're good at getting up in the morning,
I'm just too lazy.

I'm good at drawing,
But you will always be better.

Your hidden treasure is science,
But my brain gets tied in knots.

You are a footie hero,
While I run away from the ball.

Jancke Schwartz (10)
St Teresa's RC Primary School

HIDDEN TREASURE

I treasure my 1000 metre swims,
You treasure your fast running.

Your courage is a hidden treasure,
I show I'm just a mouse.

You are good at thinking quickly,
I'm as slow as a snail.

I treasure my ballet dancing,
You prefer your athletics.

Your smile is a hidden treasure,
Mine is just a silly red line.

You are good at running and hurdles,
I just knock them all over.

Your sneakiness is a hidden treasure!

Sophie Deverell (11)
St Teresa's RC Primary School

HIDDEN TREASURES

I treasure my teddy bears,
You prefer jewellery.
Your caring talent is a hidden treasure,
I show disrespect to you sometimes.
You are good at homework,
I'm not so good.
I treasure my friends,
You prefer family.
Your working talent is a hidden treasure,
I show no feeling for it.
You are good at cooking,
I'm better at talking.
I treasure the TV,
You prefer your bed.
Your maths talent is a hidden treasure,
I show little interest sometimes.
You are good at nagging,
I'm not too keen.
Love is the biggest hidden treasure in you!

Sophie Greenstreet (11)
St Teresa's RC Primary School

Hidden Treasures

I treasure my Arsenal football kit,
You prefer Man United.

You are really good at cooking,
I can't make beans on toast.

Your musical talent is a hidden treasure,
I can't play one instrument.

I treasure my Westlife CDs,
You prefer heavy metal.

Your footballing talent is a hidden treasure,
I show I can't kick a ball one inch.

I treasure my Nintendo 64,
You prefer the PlayStation 2.

You are good at reading,
I can't read one chapter.

Your golfing talent is a hidden treasure,
I can't swing a club.

Even though you're much better than me,
You're still my friend.

James Fearne (10)
St Teresa's RC Primary School

HIDDEN TREASURE

Digging, diving, looking for treasure,
Diamond rings bring you leisure.
Treasure chests full of gold,
Hiding in the sea, starting to mould.
Deep down under the sea,
Searching everywhere for that key,
I'm staring at the map
While it's sitting in my lap.
Dolphins pass, as I ride in the ocean
Reading a book about a potion,
When will I find the treasure?
Maybe if the key gets a measure.
Little fish splashing all around,
While the big fish swim on the ground.
Soon I'll get tired,
But I won't stop and get fired.
I'm eating chocolate as I go,
Keeping quiet and staying low.
Hopefully it won't take long,
For I can see a chest and a gong.
At last, I've found that hidden treasure!

Alex-Louise Cowley (11)
Smeeth CP School

HIDDEN TREASURES

Under my bed there's a trap door,
It leads me to the sea!
I often go down there for a quick swim,
To see the fish swim with glee.

But last week I had an amazing discovery.
I uncovered a ring of keys!
I searched the sea to find a lock,
But the only thing in the sea was me!

I searched and searched, swam high and low,
Then I knew it was too late.
An octopus had coiled its arms around me,
I knew I had met my fate!

I squeezed and churned and tried to squeeze free,
Just then I saw something glistening with light.
A chest with a lock to fit the key,
I tickled the octopus and then swam free.

I raced to the chest to see . . .
Gold, jewels, diamonds, rubies,
More than I could hold.
The guys at home won't believe this!

The chest was full of gold.
Just then, a light glowed around me
And to the key I grabbed hold.
I woke up in my room.

Ah! Just a dream!

Cheryl O'Brien (11)
Smeeth CP School

HIDDEN TREASURES

A treasure lies in the sea,
A large chest that needs a key.
What's in the chest is a mystery,
That's why it's deep down in the sea.
People say it's in the land,
Buried deep under the sand.
They think the chest is full of gold,
Too much for any house to hold.
People say they think they see
The hidden chest under the sea.

Samuel Hughes (10)
Smeeth CP School

HIDDEN TREASURES

Sailing, sailing across the sea,
I'm on a quest to find that key.
I've got my map,
It's on my lap,
I'm ready to tackle what lies ahead of me,
Even if it's a load of bees.
Deep, deep down under the sand
In a far, faraway land,
There lies a big treasure chest full of pure money
And if I'm lucky, a bit of honey.
I want that money, it will make me rich,
I'll be able to buy a football pitch.
I can just imagine it glistening in the sun,
Piled high in a load of iced buns.
I wonder will there be rings, bracelets,
Necklaces and lots of lovely money?
Money, money, money,
Lovely money!

Lucy Stokes (11)
Smeeth CP School

HIDDEN TREASURES

In a dark, dark wood,
In a hollow, hollow tree,
Lay the hidden treasure,
That is supposed to be there for me!
I'm starting my journey,
It's gonna be rough,
But I can fight it
I just need to be tough.
I've got my map, it's in my backpack,
Also I've got a key
That will undo the lock,
I'm getting very close. Yippee!
Oh look, it's in a hollow, hollow tree,
I've found the hidden treasure that's there for me.
Yippee!
There's gold, silver, bronze and jewellery
And it's all for me.
Yippee!

Catriona Goodman (11)
Smeeth CP School

HIDDEN TREASURE

Hidden treasure, where can it be?
In a jungle, house, maybe the deep, blue sea.
Up higher than the trees,
Or down below in the deep, blue sea.

I started walking to the shop
To get the post from Mr Pop,
There are letters all for me,
Lots of them, there are three.

I opened the letters on my lap,
I pulled it out, it's a map.
It's got a cross, a big cross too,
It's in my garden, near the loo.

Let's go and find it - dig, dig, dig,
I've banged something hard, it's a twig!
Let's keep trying, come on Mum,
Yes, we have found it. We've won!

Sinead Priestley (11)
Smeeth CP School

HIDDEN TREASURE

Peering down on my old, torn map,
Following the way, what a pleasure,
Sweating under my baseball cap,
Searching for the lost hidden treasure!
I haven't got a clue!
It's supposed to be right here,
Nodding my head I said, 'Oh dear!'
I started digging . . . *clunk.*
What was that?
I had found I had sunk,
And up I sat,
I pulled a heavy item up,
My hopes sprang,
I felt like an excited pup.
Help me, *clang!*
I've found it, look,
I'll look at it at home.
Duh, it's a book.
There I sat alone,
Peering down on my old torn map,
Following the way back, what a pleasure.
Sweating under my baseball cap,
Yes, I've found the treasure!

Mitchell Cloke (10)
Smeeth CP School

HIDDEN TREASURES

Bobbing on the sea in a big, brown boat,
Up comes an island with a very big moat.
We're capsizing and the boat doesn't float,
Swim to the island because I'm totally soaked.
How do we live in this uninhabited world?
Look over there, there's an oyster and its pearl.
Touch the oyster and the trees start to curl,
Open up a trapdoor and down I hurl.
Flying down the tunnel and my head starts to whirl,
Hit my elbow on the ground,
Oh my God! There's a load of ugly girls.
They jump on my back and with a whack, whack, whack,
The next thing I know, I'm lying on my back
In the fountain of youth and a whip goes crack,
That's the end of my dream, now let's get on track.

Hayden Waller (11)
Smeeth CP School

Hidden Treasure

I went up in the loft the other day,
As I reached the top I began to say,
What's this, a treasure chest,
Or is it just a box?

I walked up very slowly
And dust went in my eyes,
I saw this faint gold blurriness,
What is this? I sighed.

I walked up even closer
And I began to see
That it wasn't a gold treasure chest,
It was only a key!

I searched and searched
Until I found the chest.
Right beneath the chimney breast,
There was the gold chest.

I got the key out
And put it in the lock,
Twisted and twisted
Until the top popped.

Gold, silver and bronze,
Jewellery and money,
Lots and lots of things.
Going to tell my mummy!

Megan Priestley (11)
Smeeth CP School

HIDDEN TREASURES

Deep, deep under the sea,
Hidden money, gold and jewellery.
Looking hard all around,
Fighting pirates on their journey
Looking for hidden key,
Cannot find it anywhere.
Found the map long ago,
Staring at it as I go,
Look, look, what can I see?
Dolphins splashing all around.
When will I find the treasure?
You never know, I might find it in my boat.
Found the key on an island,
Found a cross, but no help there.
Rocks, rocks, all around me
In the middle of the deep, dark sea.
Digging as deep as I can,
Looking everywhere for that treasure.
Look, look, over there,
One more space to look for treasure.
Yes, at last I've found it.
Grabbing the key to open it,
It's just what I imagined,
Gold, money and jewellery.

Hollie Potter (11)
Smeeth CP School

HIDDEN TREASURE

Under the dark, salty sea,
There's a chest that needs a key,
And with that key
The chest will make you delighted
As the inside is like a night light.
I wonder where that glow comes from?
I wonder where the chest came from?
Maybe from the pirates,
Maybe from the stars?
But all I know is
That it's great!

Erik Morgan (11)
Smeeth CP School

HIDDEN TREASURES

Down, down, down in the tomb,
Step on a rock, *crack, crack, boom!*
Down comes the wall ten feet away,
Next thing I know, I'm far, far away.
Further, further, further I go,
I do not know where to go.
Suddenly I find an old map,
Under the dust is a dusty cap.

I look in my rucksack,
I find my first aid pack,
But I'm looking for food.
All I've found are things chewed.
Now I'm getting really bored,
'Help, help me!' something roared.
I followed the loud sound,
I saw a shape that was round.

I followed the long path,
There was an old bath.
I see something glimmering ahead,
But all it is, is a golden bed.
The treasure, oh yippee!
I am stuck, help me.
A boulder is coming to crush,
At it I throw an old brush.
I climb through a small gap,
And find I am on a man's lap!

James Earl (9)
Smeeth CP School

HIDDEN TREASURE

Looking in the sea,
Wondering what there could be,
Looking around through my goggles,
I saw a glowing thing. It's a golden key.
I had a map with me
But I lost it in the dead dark sea.
At last I found the treasure and grabbed it
And made a blast,
I found the surface at long last.
All I could do was take a big gasp!

Daniel Rose (11)
Smeeth CP School

HIDDEN TREASURE

In the middle of the sea,
With a map in front of me,
Searching for the treasure chest,
Finding it is my quest.
Underneath me is a giant squid,
If I carry on like this,
I'll be sure to be in Madrid.
Dead in front of me is a small piece of land,
Covered in orangey sand.
I clamber out, totally soaked
And then let go of my old, small boat.
Then as if I was talking into a microphone,
I say, I wish I was at home.
Then the ground shudders and opens with a crack,
I fall down, it's totally black.
I cry and shout
Hoping someone will hear me and get me out.
Then, as if someone turned on a light,
Everything turned terrifically bright.
Then I turn round and everything goes cold,
Right in front of me are mountains of gold.

Jamie Mansfield (10)
Smeeth CP School

THE OLD MAN AND OLD WOMAN CRIED

The old man and old woman cried
When their dog died.
They had that dog from a pup,
They watched that dog grow up.

That dog was once their friend,
Now that dog is dead.

From the house of the dead,
Laughter has gone.
To the house of the dead,
Laughter will return.

Amy Bassant (10)
Victoria Road CP School

A NEVER LOST LOSS

She was strong,
She was willing,
She was the one who plotted their escape,
She was the one who got through the back gate.

She ate my carrots
And my lettuce,
So really, she did me a favour.

But then she was lying there,
We rushed her to the vets.
Why, why? She was my pet.

Then came the phone call
A week later,
It was them, I should have been expecting,
But I was not.
It was the vet,
No longer did I have a pet

It didn't really sink in,
Well, until night.
It was like having a poisonous bite.

I stood at the top of the stairs
And screamed with all my might.
I screamed as loud as thunder,
'Snuffles!'

I was terrified,
I'd lost some of my heart,
In fact, I was horrified.

It's now I suffer,
I really can't stand,
It's like being banned,
It's . . .
I have to live my life without Snuffles!

Grace Cradduck (9)
Victoria Road CP School

A BANANA SPLIT

First, I freshly peel its yellow skin
And almost cut it in half.
Then put it into a bowl.

Now drown it in whipped cream,
Put on the melted chocolate,
Then add five strawberries.

Add sprinkles,
Take it to table 14
And get ready for a *banana split!*

Kristian Assirati (10)
Victoria Road CP School

MY POOR RABBIT

This is a story of my bunny,
She was like no other.
All my family loved her,
She didn't have a brother.

Until one day when she was ill,
We took her to the vets.
We were all upset,
I had some bets.

Until a few days,
We were in tears.
We all loved her.
I couldn't believe it, she was only two years.

Laura Love (10)
Victoria Road CP School

RABBITS

R abbits are cute but
A s cheeky as can be.
B rambles are prickly,
B ut rabbits are cheeky.
I t's quite funny
T hat they're bigger than you think,
S o that's why I like rabbits.

Sophie Ross (9)
Victoria Road CP School

THE CARROT

As I pull out a knife,
I sharpen it in front of the creature.
As I strike it on its fuzzy, green hair,
I pour some water into a pan,
I wait for it to boil.
Shriek!
It's boiled, I throw the creature in.
I thought to myself that night,
I just killed a carrot.

Darryl Mills (10)
Victoria Road CP School

THE ELEGY OF THE APPLE

I took the skin off with a knife,
'Help me, please.'
I cut the middle out,
'Help me, please.'
I ate it.
The apple was dead.

George Knight (9)
Victoria Road CP School

Elegy On The Death Of Cream!

As my brother ripped open the packet
And shoved it in the bowl,
He put water on it. 'Watch out, you could drown it.'
He whipped it until it cried.
My brother went out of the room,
I picked up the bowl,
I looked inside
And I saw white blood pouring out.
It was dead!

Joshua Oakden-Telfer (10)
Victoria Road CP School

PAST THE CLOUDS

Past the clouds,
Beyond the sun and the rainbow,
There lies a world
With flowers and trees,
Fresh water,
Shrubs and vegetables,
A place beyond this world,
Much better than ours,
With milk and honey.

Liam Archer (10)
Victoria Road CP School

MOON

Moonlight, moonlight,
Shines, oh so bright
Through the gloomy night.
You're shaped like a gun,
You're firing a silver light
Down to Earth.

Moonlight, moonlight,
Your colour is so soft,
You look so smooth.
At night I hear you say,
'Goodnight,' as I snuggle
Down in bed.

Jessica Proctor (9)
Victoria Road CP School

MY NEW HOUSE

We've sold our flat,
We're on our way
To a house with a garden,
It's not too far away.

I'll get a room of my own
That I won't have to share
With my brother and sister
And their teddy bears.

I will keep it nice and tidy
So my mum won't have to moan.
I can shut the door and off I go
Into a world of my own.

Elend Apps (9)
Victoria Road CP School

MY GUY

My little brother, my little brother,
He's my best little guy ever.
I enjoy playing with my little guy,
My guy,
I love my little guy.
He enjoys school a lot,
My guy,
He enjoys eating pie, my guy.
But my guy sometimes doesn't like eating pies.
He's very, very funny, my guy,
My little brother.

Christopher Stow (9)
Victoria Road CP School

My Dad

This is a poem about my dad,
Who sometimes is quite mad.
I like to practice my dances,
But he pulls funny faces.
Sometimes he takes us swimming,
But he doesn't like my singing.
He can scream and shout,
And likes to muck about.
My dad is the best,
Better than the rest!

Jemma Wead (8)
Victoria Road CP School

MY DOG CHARLIE

I have a little dog and Charlie is his name,
He does some funny things, I think he is insane.
He doesn't like his bath and causes lots of trouble,
But when I'm having my bath, he tries to eat the bubbles.
He's always pleased to see me when I come through the door,
He gets so very excited and knocks me on the floor.
He gets up in the morning and has a wander round,
But when there's nothing happening, he doesn't stick around.
From side to side he turns his head and goes straight back to bed.

Samuel Tutt (8)
Victoria Road CP School

MERMAIDS

Under the sea you can see
Lots of mermaids swimming about,
Waving their tails high up in the sky
Like a diamond in the sky.
Sitting on a rock and waving their tails.
Are they really real?

Nurjahan Begum (9)
Victoria Road CP School

MY BROTHER

My brother is really cute
And sometimes he can be a brute.
He likes meat,
He thinks the world's at his feet.
He is so cute,
That's my brother.

Troi Cozens (8)
Victoria Road CP School

THE SUN

The sun is like a gigantic fireball,
The sun is very bright,
The sun is like a torch shining through the clouds,
The sun is boiling water,
If you touch the sun you will be burnt.
The sun is a mystery,
The sun is nice for playing games,
The sun is bigger than the BFG.
When it rains and the sun comes out
It will make a rainbow.

Joseph Dibley (8)
Victoria Road CP School

APPLES

An apple is so sweet
And it's juicy too.
It's round like the Earth,
Remember to twist the stalk just in case.
Be careful because you might eat a pip.
I don't like the skin so I peel it off.
It's a bit like a pear, but it's rounded at the top
And it's round like an orange,
But they're a bit bumpier than an apple.
And remember, don't forget the pips!

Siân Clampitt (9)
Victoria Road CP School

BOOKS

Books are fun, fun, fun,
Some are scary,
Some are fun
And my favourites are the mysterious ones.
I love books, books, books,
Scary, funny and mysterious ones!

Oliver Rich (8)
Victoria Road CP School

MY FRIEND THE MOON

You are always watching me.
Sometimes I see all your face,
Sometimes only half.

You can be different colours,
Sometimes pale blue or bright silver,
But you're always watching me.

Some people say you're made of cheese,
Some people say a man lives there,
But all I see is the brightest light.

Your light helps people in the dark.
You go to bed in daytime and get up at night.
I see the brightest light, my friend, the moon.

Rebecca Dodd (9)
Victoria Road CP School

THE SEA

The sea is beautiful,
The sea makes me feel plucky,
The sea glitters when the sun shines,
The sea gives silent breezes that are so smooth,
The sea makes me feel cosy,
The sea makes me go to sleep,
The sea is so gentle,
The seawater is wavy,
The sea makes me joyful.

Shaker Miah (9)
Victoria Road CP School

FOOTBALL TEAMS

Football is a sport,
But who do you support?
Man U or Chelsea, even,
Who do you support?

I support Man U,
Or Chelsea, even,
Who would you support?
None of them.
I support Liverpool,
Liverpool are good,
But they can be thrashed.

By who?
Man U or Chelsea, even.
You should support someone else.

All right, I support
Man U or Chelsea, even,
So who do you support?
Liverpool!

Nicholas Webb (8)
Victoria Road CP School

THE MOON MAN

Moon man way up there, is it cold?
The moon is lovely and silver.
Moon man way up there, is the moon shaped as a banana?
You light me the way home with your glistening light.
When I go to bed, I hear you say, 'Goodnight!'
Do you really say it?
Well, I'm not sure if you're up there in the gloomy night.
Anyway, if you're up there,
'Goodnight, moon man, goodnight.'

Katie Bishop (9)
Victoria Road CP School

CROCODILE

Crocodile, crocodile, big snappy jaws,
You find them in lakes and ponds.
If you go near him, he'll crunch your fingers off,
Don't go near a crocodile if you've got your shoes off,
Because if you do, you will get told to get out,
So don't go in, just stay out of the crocodile den,
Then you're safe from them.
Crocodiles, vicious, cheeky and sometimes tired,
They'll bite you to pieces,
But take your shoes off first, so *keep out!*

Natasha Fletcher (9)
Victoria Road CP School

ELEGY OF AN ONION

It is so sad that Mr Onion died the other day.
Here is the story!

When the onion got pulled out of the ground,
He was placed in a basket.
A big, giant hand took him prisoner for five minutes.
Ten minutes later he was in a bowl
Being crushed with his worst enemies.
When in the frying pan,
He shrivelled up like a prune!
It suddenly occurred to me that the onion was dead!

Louise Morgan (9)
Victoria Road CP School

MY SISTER

My sister
Is really cute,
She has
Lovely brown hair
And wonderful
Brown eyes.
Sometimes I
Miss her,
But sometimes
I hate her.
She pulls
My hair.
She cries
And she
Comes in
My room.
I love
And hate
My sister.

Elizabeth McAdams (9)
Victoria Road CP School

MY SCHOOL

My school is big on the outside
But small on the inside.
I find it quite strange sometimes.
Sometimes I think it's haunted myself.
Mr Dawson, our deputy head, is very strict but funny.
When you look at him, you sometimes nearly jump out of your skin,
Well, I do anyway.
What isn't fair is that he gets to eat crisps at play time and we don't.
Mr Guthrie, our head, is not like Mr Dawson.
Mr Guthrie is very, very strict,
You wouldn't want to take a wrong turn with him.
He'll eat you for dinner.
Mr Dawson has a very big appetite,
He eats bigger things than me for breakfast,
But my school is great,
I have never gotten into trouble, unlike some people,
And that's how I'm going to stay!

Sarah Bohill (9)
Victoria Road CP School